THE COMMUNIST PROGRAM
FOR WORLD CONQUEST

CONSULTATION WITH
GEN. ALBERT C. WEDEMEYER
UNITED STATES ARMY

HOUSE OF REPRESENTATIVES

EIGHTY-FIFTH CONGRESS
SECOND SESSION
JANUARY 21, 1958

Printed for the use of the Committee on
Un-American Activities

2

COMMITTEE ON UN-AMERICAN ACTIVITIES UNITED STATES HOUSE OF REPRESENTATIVES

SYNOPSIS

Economic and psychological weapons rather than the launching of a third world war comprise the current Communist program for world conquest, General Albert C. Wedemeyer warned in a consultation with the Committee on Un-American Activities. One of the top strategic planners of World War II, General Wedemeyer was present at many international conferences as adviser to the President. He attended the conferences in Washington, London, Cairo, Quebec, and Casablanca before going to China as theater commander in 1944. "They (the Communists) are attaining their objectives without the use of military force," General Wedemeyer said if I were the senior planner in the Soviet hierarchy, I would advise Khrushchev: "Continue to do exactly what you are doing now. Do not involve the Soviet Union in a major war but employ the satellites in brush fires or limited wars against our enemies, the capitalist countries. Continue penetration economically and psychologically, utilize economic or military aid to as many countries in the world as possible. They can be made indebted to the Soviet, and if not loyal, at least they will not be opposed to the Communist movement."

"I do not believe that they intend to precipitate an all-out war," he declared.

I have not felt that war was imminent at any time since World War II even when there were incidents that might have easily touched off a world struggle. You may recall the Berlin airlift, for example. There have been many other incidents that could have started a war if the Soviets had any desire to start an all-out war. They will continue to spread communism utilizing economic and psychological weapons.

General Wedemeyer warned that the Soviet Union today has "greater military capabilities than do we." This has been true ever since the end of World War II When we emasculated our military forces and at the same time permitted the Soviet to retain a massive army, a big navy, and air force. At one time we had a technological advantage, particularly in the atomic weapon field, which served as a deterrent.

General Wedemeyer expressed the view that it is now too late for the West on the Soviet timetable for world domination, but he added: However, I am not completely pessimistic about our chances
To recover a sufficiently strong strategic posture vis-à-vis the Soviet. If we make a careful analysis of all of the countries which endanger our position, evaluate their capabilities and their limitations, and then determine how much assistance, realistic or passive, that we might expect from allies, and finally consider our own potential strength, I think that we would find our position in the world is not without hope, in fact we would be most optimistic if we could foresee the coordinated employment of all the positive forces that we have on our side to counter our potential enemies and to overcome obstacles offered by them to the attainment of our objectives.

I have confidence in American ingenuity, in our courage,

and in our capacity to plan intelligently if we are only provided the direction from responsible leaders. But we must bring about concerted action to attain our goals and stop the indiscriminate and uncoordinated use of our political, economic, psychological, and military forces.

General Wedemeyer continued we have wonderful opportunities in the struggle against communism if we would use our economic weapon intelligently. In helping other peoples economically we should be careful not to do so on a charity basis. Such an approach makes the recipient or beneficiary lose his self-respect. Outright charity undermines the moral fiber of an individual or of a nation. But we can provide economic or technical aid in such a manner as to enable the recipient peoples to help themselves and even make it possible for them to return or pay back our largess. One cannot help but pay tribute to the brave and self-respecting Finns. They were the only people who paid their World War I debt to the United States. All other so called allies, the recipients of our loans and aid in other forms, reneged.

He cautioned, however, that I would not vote one penny to any country unless I had evidence of their good faith and of their unswerving loyalty in the cooperative effort with us toward the attainment of common objectives; one important one, of course, is protecting the Free World against the scourge of communism. I am not suggesting that each one of these countries to whom we give military and economic aid should have exactly the same objectives in the international field, but I would insist that their objectives must be compatible with our own. In other words, if the British insist on trading with Red China and thus strengthening the Communists who present a grave danger to United States interests, then I would discontinue military or economic aid to the British. When I make a statement like that, Britishers and American "one-worlders" will say that they are not trading in strategic items. When they use the term "strategic items," they mean, of course, airplanes, tanks, ammunition, I presume. But I insist that any item of trade-a spool of thread, wheat, automobiles, or coffee-assists the economy of Red China.

I believe in denying those areas under Communist rule any economic or military assistance. Furthermore I would break off diplomatic relations with them.

In suggesting these ideas to the committee, I wish to emphasize that I am not an isolationist. No country can isolate itself from the world today. If this be a fact, the United States should participate in international developments and relations with intelligence always mindful of the fact that we must be actuated by self-respect.

In other words, every step that we take should protect our security and our economy. Let us be realistic and understand that all other countries conduct their foreign policies in that manner.

Despite the apparent changes in Soviet tactics, the ultimate objectives of communism are unchangeable, General Wedemeyer declared: The objectives of the

Soviet are clearly stated in the Communist Manifesto and again developed in the two volumes of Das Kapital by Karl Marx. These Soviet objectives are available for the public to read. Hitler announced to the world in the same unmistakable manner his objectives in a book, Mein Kampf. But no one paid any attention to Hitler's attempt to warn the world of his intentions. I wonder if we are paying sufficient attention to the Communist objectives?

The overall, clearly announced objective of international communism is to free the proletariat from exploitation by the bourgeoisie. The masses are to be protected from the scheming capitalists. The world is to be communized.

There is no possibility of compromise with the Soviet Union and world communism, General Wedemeyer asserted, inasmuch as "kill, lie, distort, torture-all are fully justified in the Soviet conscience because they are so dedicated to the attainment of Marxian, Leninist, or Stalinist objectives."

THE COMMUNIST PROGRAM FOR WORLD CONQUEST
TUESDAY, JANUARY 21, 1958
UNITED STATES HOUSE OF REPRESENTATIVES,
COMMITTEE ON UN-AMERICAN ACTIVITIES,
Washington, D. C.
The Committee on Un-American Activities met, pursuant to call, at 10 a. m., in room 225, Old House Office Building, Washington, D. C., Hon. Clyde Doyle, presiding .

Committee members present:
Representatives Francis E. Walter, of Pennsylvania, chairman of the committee (appearance as noted); Clyde Doyle, of California; Bernard W. Kearney, of New York ; and Gordon H. Scherer, of Ohio.

Staff members present: Richard Arens, staff director, and William F. Heimlich, consultant.

Mr. DOYLE. In the absence of the distinguished committee chairman, Francis E. Walter, temporarily, I am calling the meeting to order. We are favored this morning with the testimony of Gen. Albert C. Wedemeyer. We appreciate very much, General, your being with us. What is the first order of business, Mr. Arens?

Mr. ARENS: If you please, Mr. Chairman, I would suggest that the general might for our record, at this time, give a brief sketch of his career.

Mr. KEARNEY. May I interrupt, please? Is it necessary that the general be sworn?

Mr. ARENS. It has not been the practice of the committee to swear persons who are in consultation on international communism as distinct from persons who might be testifying for the purpose of identifying persons.

Mr. KEARNEY. In other words, you mean the general is not going to take the Fifth Amendment.

Mr. ARENS. I do not anticipate so.

General WEDEMEYER. I would gladly be sworn if you want me to be.

Mr. KEARNEY. No.

Mr. DOYLE. I think no doubt the record will show the committee members present.

Mr. ARENS. I respectfully suggest, General, you might give us the highlights of your most distinguished career.

GEN. ALBERT C. WEDEMEYER, UNITED STATES ARMY (RETIRED)

General WEDEMEYER. My name is Albert C. Wedemeyer. I am a retired general of the United States Army. My career in the Army included cadet service at West Point, lieutenant in June 1919, and the usual company and field grades in the infantry and finally reached general officer rank in 1942. After I completed 2 years at the United States Army staff school at Fort Leavenworth, I was assigned as a student by the War Department to the German War College located in Berlin, Germany. This experience of 2 1/2 years as a student and resident in Germany greatly stimulated my interest in international developments.

Mr. SCHERER. What year was that, General Wedemeyer?

General WEDEMETER. I was in Germany from July 1936 to October 1938, which of course were very eventful years in central Europe. During that period nazism was at its peak in power. While in Germany I met many of the Nazi leaders, including Hess, Goering, ,and Goebbels, and of course I was thrown in contact even more with the senior military leaders as well as the military officers at the German War College, both students and instructors. For example, Jodl, who later became Hitler's strategic adviser with the rank of colonel general, was my instructor. Count Klaus von Stauffenburg, the officer who placed a bomb under a' desk in an abortive attempt to kill Hitler on July 20, 1944, was my classmate in the German War College. Von Stauffenberg was a very unusual man-intelligent, courageous and I considered him a good friend. All of these contacts and the opportunity of reading and hearing about nazism, fascism, and communism aroused my curiosity. I tried to understand the conditions that stimulated or generated those "isms," and made it possible for their proponents to gain the attention and ofttimes the fanatic support of so many people. Obviously these were unique opportunities to observe and experience momentous events leading up to World War II. The instruction at the German War College was far superior to that which I experienced at our own staff school at Leavenworth. The students in Germany were required to study history and were thoroughly grounded in the fundamentals of military science, tactics, and strategy. At the conclusion of my service in Germany, I submitted an official report to the War Department. The Chief of Staff of our Army at that time was Gen. Maim* Craig.

Mr. SCHERER. What was your rank at that time?

General WEDEMEYER. I was a captain. I was 17 years a lieutenant. This may seem unusual but in prewar days promotion was very slow. After World War II began, promotion was rapid. Upon my return from duty in Germany, I was assigned to troop duty at Fort Benning and then after 1 year there I was brought into the War Plans Division of the General Staff in Washington. In this assignment I assisted in the preparation of our strategy, and during the first few years of the war I attended world conferences in London, Washington, Casablanca, Cairo, and Quebec with General Marshall. In September 1943 I was assigned to duty in the Southeast Asia Command with Admiral Mountbatten and then a year later, 1944, I was sent to China to relieve General Stilwell as theater commander. I held that post until May of 1946 when the theater was disbanded. I returned to the States ostensibly to be Ambassador to China. Mr. Truman had asked me to accept that post after General Hurley resigned in the fall of 1945. General Marshall urged me to do so and I agreed. However, the news concerning my prospective appointment as Ambassador to China leaked in that part of the world. General Marshall at the time was conducting delicate negotiations involving Nationalists and Communists, and apparently he felt that the news of my appointment was militating against the success of his negotiations, particularly because the Communists objected violently. Accordingly General Marshall radioed to President Truman requesting the appointment of Dr, Leighton Stuart, an American missionary living in China. In that radiogram he asked that General Wedemeyer be notified that he would be appointed later.

Mr. ARENS. General, would you give us a thumbnail sketch of the functions you performed in World War II in strategy and policy for the global operations of the United States?

General WEDEMEYER. Yes ; shortly after my return from Europe and immediately prior to World War II, I was assigned to the General Staff, War Plans Division, and by the spring of 1942 I was put in charge of the strategic policy and plans group. This group had the responsibility of conducting strategic studies, evolving plans for the employment of our forces and coordinating our war effort with allies. Our objective was to insure that the military effort would protect America's interests and accomplish our objectives at home and abroad. To state this point in another way, I felt that it was very important at war's end to insure that Anglo-American forces would be occupying most of Western Europe and the Balkans. Some of us recognized the danger of international communism and, although the Soviet Union was an ally, we wanted to insure that the Communist forces could not fill the vacua created by killing and destruction during the course of the war throughout Europe. Most of us interpreted nazism as a strong nationalist movement whereas we felt that communism was an international movement supported by a worldwide conspiratorial effort. As we viewed it then, nazism would take unfair advantage, would subvert or conquer areas in their narrow, strongly nationalistic interests, whereas communism was worldwide in scope and visualized the enslavement or conquering of all peoples.

Mr. ARENS. With that brief personal sketch on the record, may we ask you to give your characterization or appraisal of the struggle of the world today as between the East and the West?

General WEDEMEYER. In the first instance I think that the West is overshadowed by international communism. I think that communism is gaining instead of losing strength in the world. You are familiar with history and therefore all of you realize that a struggle between nations and peoples has always been going on. There is nothing new about such struggle, but we Americans after World War II were either naive, or too trusting. There is considerable evidence to prove that there were malicious influences in key places of our Government. But any one or a combination of these circumstances permitted a critical situation to develop after World War II, namely, the Soviet emerged all powerful-and our war aims for which we sacrificed so much were not accomplished. We continued to give vast sums of money and materials and even our moral support after the war to the Soviet Union and her satellites. In other words, communism gained its position as a world power through our own lack of appreciation of the dangers inherent in communism. You gentlemen may have more knowledge than I do about the responsibility for these developments. Today communism, in my judgment, is increasing in its influence and strength, not only in the military field but in scientific accomplishments. Sputnik is just one example. Several years ago they had a fighter plane-the MIG-15-that was superior to our Saber Jets in Korea. These planes could outmaneuver our fighter aircraft and reach higher altitudes. Recently they developed an icebreaker with atomic power. In their schooling, their educational system, one cannot help but be impressed by the number of engineers and applied scientists they have trained. In pure science as well as applied science they seem to be ahead of us. The Soviets have been improving steadily and they have even forged ahead in many fields - education, production, technology, sciences, athletics, for example. If I were the senior planner in the Soviet hierarchy, I would advise Khrushchev: "Continue to do exactly what you are doing now. Do not involve the Soviet Union in a major war but employ the satellites in brush fires or limited wars against our enemies, the capitalist countries. Continue penetration, economically and psychologically, utilize economic or military aid to as many countries in the world as possible. They can be made indebted to the Soviet, and if not loyal, at least they will not be opposed to the Communist movement." One could cite numerous examples of their clever use of the economic aid as a strategic weapon.

Mr. ARENS. As we look at the other side of the coin, what do you believe to be the global strategy of the Soviets?

General WEDEMEYER. I do not believe that they intend to precipitate an all-out war. I have not felt that war was imminent at any time since World War II even when there were incidents that might have easily touched off a world struggle. You may recall the Berlin airlift, for example. There have been many other incidents that could have started a war if the Soviets had any desire to start an all-out war. They will continue to spread communism utilizing economic and psychological weapons.

Mr. SCHERER. Mr. Chairman, may I ask a question that I think is pertinent right at this point?

Mr. DOYLE. Yes.

Mr. SCHERER. You say Russia is not interested in precipitating-or you do not believe they will precipitate a world war or struggle. Is it because they have made so much progress without such a war that you do not believe that they will precipitate us into another world war?

General WEDEMEYER. Yes; I think that is a sound conclusion. May I just explain to you my concept of strategy, in lay language? The term "strategy" disturbs many people just as the word "propaganda" does. I define "strategy" as the art and science of using all of a nation's available resources to accomplish national objectives. There are four major categories of resources: political, economic, psychological, and military. If the first three of these resources-that is, political, economic, and psychological-are employed intelligently and boldly in consonance with a well-thought-out plan, it may never be necessary to use actively our military force. Obviously that is exactly what we should do at all times-prevent war and yet accomplish our national aims. But we must retain military force-appropriate in strength and composition to our possible need in emergency. In our communities we employ the police to maintain order and to protect people who respect the law against those who would violate it. In the international arena we must do likewise, only calling on the military when all other means fail to accomplish our purposes.

Mr. SCHERER. The Soviets have been very successful in using these first three resources.

General WEDEMEYER. In my opinion, yes.

Mr. ARENS. I think you may want to clarify the record. The Congressman asked you about a war. I am sure he had in mind a shooting war in which guns and missiles would be employed. Is there any doubt in your mind but what the Soviet Union and her satellites are presently engaged in war with the United States as their No.1 target?

General WEDEMEYER. We associate shooting and the employment of military force with war. When we employ the other three resources political, economic, and psychological - I term such employment not in the sense of war but as a struggle going on with other nations.

Mr. ARENS. What is the objective of the Soviet Union and its satellites?

General WEDEMEYER. The objectives of the Soviet are clearly stated in the Communist Manifesto and again developed in the two volumes of Das Kapital by Karl Marx. These Soviet objectives are available for the public to read. Hitler announced to the world in the same unmistakable manner his objectives in a book, Mein Kampf. But no one paid any attention to Hitler's attempt to warn the world of his intentions. I wonder if we are paying sufficient attention to the Communist objectives? The overall, clearly announced objective of international communism is to free the proletariat from exploitation by the bourgeoisie. The masses are to be protected from the scheming capitalists. The world is to be communized.

Mr. KEARNEY. General, you answered, as I understand it, that Russia at the present time does not want to have a shooting war?

General WEDEMEYER. I do not believe they do, sir.

Mr. KEARNEY. Is that due to the fact that Russia is obtaining its objectives without a shooting war, or is it due to the fact that they do not trust their satellites?

General WEDEMEYER. It is due primarily to the fact that they are attaining their objectives without the use of military force. It is true that they are compelled to accept reverses at times in particular areas but they invariably are making headway in some other areas. Furthermore, although they may suffer a setback in a specific area, later on they conduct their plans in such a way as to recover their losses and actually make gains in that same area .

Mr. KEARNEY. Then may I ask you, in case of a shooting war, in your opinion could Russia depend upon her satellites in view of the riots in Poland the East German June 1953 riots, and the recent Hungarian revolution?

General WEDEMEYER. It is my opinion that the Soviet Union could not depend upon her satellites or upon the millions of oppressed peoples within her own borders in the event of a war, which would produce opportunities to defect with a chance of success. Under such conditions there would be opportunities for the western nations to exploit defections that occur in the satellite countries and even in Russia. In connection with the attitude or the possible defection of peoples behind the Iron Curtain, may I suggest, General Kearney, that we consider extending our own efforts to bring about and support such defections. For example, we are expending billions of dollars for weapons that will kill and destroy. We are assembling the best brains in the country to insure that we surpass other countries, particularly the Soviet Union, in the development of ultra destructive weapons. But I, personally, would like concurrently to recommend the collection of brains and the expenditure of effort- billions of dollars, if necessary- to find out what we can do to reach the minds of peoples behind the Iron

Curtain, to win their loyalties and sympathetic understanding, and thus avoid the possibility of a destructive thermonuclear war. There are two points that we must make crystal clear to our potential enemies, neutrals, and friends: First, that we are sincere in our desire for peace and in our willingness to cooperate realistically to protect the freedoms and improve opportunities of the individual of any clime, race, or creed; and second, that we are determined to use every resource at our command to destroy communism, or any other "ism" that jeopardizes peace in the world. Unless we undertake successfully such an approach to our international problems, civilization as we know it will be retarded at least a thousand years. Let's put constructive ideas instead of hydrogen bombs in the nose cone of our missiles.

Mr. KEARNEY. With that I thoroughly agree. When you speak as you do about the best brains now trying to figure out ways and means of bringing into being weapons that can win a shooting war, we have only to go back to your original statement that after World War II we just practically disbanded the greatest fighting force in the world while Russia, without the loss of a Russian soldier, took over about 800 million people.

General WEDEMEYER. General Kearney, we had plenty of evidence before and during World War II of the recalcitrance of the Soviet Union, of their motives, and their unscrupulous arrogant method. They at all times had their selfish interests in mind and would not cooperate except when it would be advantageous to them, and to them alone. As a strategic planner on the General Staff in Washington during the early days of the war, I frequently contacted Russian representatives and asked them where, when, and how they planned to use the equipment that they were demanding or requisitioning from us for example, airplanes, tanks, guns, thousands of tons of equipment of all kinds. We were pouring war supplies into the Soviet Union, often at great sacrifice to our own forces which we were generating here at home and preparing for shipment to prospective areas of employment against the enemy. But General Kearney, the Russian representatives would not cooperate with regard to explaining where and when they intended to use the munitions we were shipping to them. In fact they were very cool and even suspicious when one approached them concerning any problem. They refused to give any indication of their prospective pans in fighting the Germans yet they were supposed to be an ally. I tried to explain carefully my purpose in determining where, how, and when they would use the tanks, airplanes, and so forth, against the common enemy. For example, I had to recommend to General Marshall priorities for allocation of the equipment, not only to Russia but to England and other allies. If England could use the tanks more effectively and more quickly against the enemy, it seemed to me that she should get higher priority. I mentioned my difficulty in this regard to General Marshall and to Harry Hopkins, as well as to others in positions of responsibility but got nowhere. One of the ablest men in the State Department, Mr. Loy Henderson, considered an expert in dealing with Russia, attempted to help me. He recognized the importance of allocating our war materials on the basis of its most effective use against the enemy. But the Soviet representatives would not cooperate in any respect.

Mr. ARENS. May I ask you, General, concerning the instruments of national policy which you described: Do you feel that the Soviet Union uses these instruments effectively in its designs for world conquest?

General WEDEMEYER. Yes, I do. They use economic and psychological weapons most effectively. We know that the Soviet Union does not honor any treaty or agreement unless advantage accrues to them. They have been very clever in penetrating in various countries the Department of Interior, which is really the department responsible for internal security matters. After the Communists obtain control of the secret police and administrative setup of the security department, they can easily take over the government by intimidating or removing responsible officials in other departments. Czechoslovakia is an example of this technique, but similar tactics were employed in Hungary and throughout the Balkan State. Lithuania, Estonia, and Latvia were overpowered quickly and brought into the Soviet Union against the will of the inhabitants. We have wonderful opportunities in the struggle against communism if we would use our economic weapon intelligently. In helping other peoples economically we should be careful not to do so on a charity basis. Such an approach makes the recipient or beneficiary lose his self-respect. Outright charity undermines the moral fiber of an individual or of a nation. But we can provide economic or technical aid in such a manner as to enable the recipient peoples to help themselves and even make it possible for them to return or pay back our largess. One cannot help but pay tribute to the brave and self-respecting Finns. They were the only people who paid their World War I debt to the United States. All other so-called allies, the recipients of our loans and aid in other forms, reneged.

Mr. KEARNEY. And we kicked the Finns in the pants later.

General WEDEMEYER. Yes, we did, very much as we turned our backs on loyal allies, the Nationalist Chinese, after World War II. May I give you a concrete example of the manner in which the Russians use the economic weapon in their campaign to control and communize other countries? Some few years back the Egyptians wanted to buy wheat from the United States. The Egyptian Ambassador negotiated here in Washington with appropriate officials. Nothing came of the negotiations and as time went on the Egyptian Government continued to prompt its Ambassador to do something about it. However, he was unable to get a definitive answer from anyone in authority in the State Department. The Egyptians were perfectly willing to pay for the wheat in dollars and they sorely needed it for their people. Finally in some unknown manner the Soviet Union learned of the Egyptian attempt to get wheat from the United States. This was not understood by the Egyptian Ambassador or his Government for all of the negotiations had been conducted in the utmost secrecy with United States officials. In a short time the Soviet Union offered the Egyptian Government all the wheat it would require, and at first there were no strings attached. Gradually, however, the quality of the wheat deteriorated and there were other disagreeable features injected by the Soviet Union. This cooperative action on the part of the Soviet Union was known by all of the Egyptians and was, of course, interpreted as a friendly gesture by them. Further, the Soviet Union agents in Egypt made it their duty to insure that all of the Egyptians were told that the United States refused to sell wheat to the Egyptian Government and the Soviet Union voluntarily came forward and provided the wheat. Then we wonder why people do not know about, or seem to misinterpret, our actions and policies. Another feature of the Soviet tactics in using the economic weapon before Khrushchev or Bulganin visit a foreign country, the Soviet Union usually makes some favorable economic gesture to that country. Then they insure that all of the people are informed of the great Communist largess-the role of helping the poor people. When Khrushchev or Bulganin arrive, of course they are the recipients of praise, gratitude, and extraordinary manifestation of friendship. On the other hand, we Americans, apparently, do nothing to inform people of the aid that we are giving to them directly or indirectly through their government. The timing of our aid apparently is never coordinated with a visit of one of our officials. It seems to me that we have no plan in this connection and there apparently is no agency of the Government responsible for coordination of our efforts in the political, economic, and psychological fields. I think it is contemplated that the National Security Council exercise overall supervision of these activities which we have been discussing this morning, particularly the coordination of military and economic aid to friendly nations, the worldwide information program, including the dissemination of overt and covert propaganda, and finally the use of trade agreements and political alliances to strengthen our position vis-à-vis potential enemies. But I do not feel that the National Security Council is the proper agency for such supervision because it comprises individuals who have great responsibilities in other areas. T hey simply cannot devote the time necessary to function properly in the National Security Council. For example, the President, the Secretary of State, the Secretary of Defense and the head of CIA all have day-to-day administrative responsibilities which preclude their participation in the planning and coordinating of our worldwide policies and actions. On the other hand, the Soviet Union apparently has an excellent plan and organization through which it is enjoying great success all over the world. The Russians are not 10-foot men and they have their weaknesses as well as their strong points. We must not overemphasize their strength. We are just as intelligent as they are. I think we are in a weaker position today principally because we have been naïve and trusting, as well as somewhat apathetic toward events occurring in other parts of the world.

Mr. KEARNEY. That is true, General, but at the same time it is my humble opinion that Russia has an objective in mind. It seems to me, and I may be totally wrong, that most of our people who are engaged in office work are simply there because they are drawing pay. There is no plan as you say. This goes way back to the days of UNRRA. We have never been credited with doing the right thing in the right manner.

General WEDEMEYER. I agree. Immediately after the war I saw material out in China sent there by the United States for distribution by UNRRA to help the Chinese. The markings which would indicate that this economic aid came from the United States had been obliterated, and the Russians had put markers on the containers to deceive the Chinese people into thinking that they, the Soviet Union, sent the aid. Later, when I was in Iran, I learned officially that although the United States was furnishing large quantities of milk for the Iranian children, the Soviet Union had given the people of Iran the impression that it was the Communists who were sympathetic to the needs of the masses of people and it was the Soviet Union that had sent the milk to their children. I think this pattern was followed throughout the world. We never received credit for the great humanitarian effort that we made to restore and rehabilitate the war-devastated areas. If there had not been an aggressive country like the Soviet Union with world-conquering objectives, of course, we would not have been presented with the problem. We must wake up and insure that our traditional generous efforts to help others are understood and that the Soviet Union does not get credit for the sacrifices that we are making.

Mr. KEARNEY. Is it because we have people in our agencies overseas who do not seem to care so long as they have a ob or are being entertained and wined and dined, or is it because the State Department here does not put its foot down and does not have an overall plan?

General WEDEMEYER. Of course, a breakdown in the functioning of an organization is usually attributed to the responsible leaders. In my judgment our leaders have not been trained properly in international negotiations and operations. They are just as worthy, honest, and efficient as they are in any other country but they lack proper training and guidance. When I first came in contact with the British during the war, I was greatly impressed with their unanimity of purpose, their loyalty to definite objectives or policies of the British Commonwealth. No matter where I went in the world this was true. The British representatives always seemed to be knowledgeable about their

Commonwealth policies and they loyally supported them. There was a continuity and a high degree of coordination in all of their policies and actions in the international field. This was not true in our own case. We Americans were not sure about our country's objectives. There was a lack of coordination between the economic the political, the military, and the psychological efforts being made by various American departments and agencies.

Mr. SCHERER. You mean among the Americans in the administration of our foreign-aid projects?

General WEDEMEYER. Yes, sir. I definitely include the administration of our foreign aid. Also, Mr. Congressman, I mentioned earlier that I tried to compel an ally (the Soviet Union) to explain how they were going to use, and when they planned to do so, the equipment that they were receiving from us. I tried to compel the Soviet representatives to tell me but they refused. I could not obtain the support of people higher up in our own Government in this regard. We had men in our own military forces training with wooden guns because we had shipped so many of the real weapons to the Soviet Union. We had a great shortage of tanks and other weapons which were needed urgently by our troops undergoing training. Yet we were shipping almost indiscriminately and without obtaining information as to their use-tons and tons of weapons to the Soviet Union.

Mr. SCHERER. When you use the term "allies," do you mean Russia or all of our allies?

General WEDEMEYER. I mean all of our allies, Mr. Congressman, including the British who were also making demands upon us for equipment. In the early days of the war, they too were getting huge quantities of critical materiel from us and there was little or no coordination concerning how and when they were going to use such equipment against the enemy. Later we were able to obtain better cooperation from the British but the Soviet Union never did cooperate as a loyal ally should in this or any other regard.

Mr. ARENS. In the light of recent events, must we assume that the Soviet Union has reached parity with the United States in military capabilities?

General WEDEMEYER. I think the Soviet Union has greater military capabilities than do we. This has been true ever since the end of World War II when we emasculated our military forces and at the same time permitted the Soviet to retain a massive army, a big navy, and air force. At one time we had a technological advantage, particularly in the atomic weapon field, which served as a deterrent.

Mr. ARENS. How do these comparative capabilities affect our relationship with allied nations with whom we have mutual defense treaties in all parts of the world?

General WEVEMEYER. This situation should make our allies rather reluctant; at least it suggests possible dangerous implications of cooperating with the United States, with reference to accepting American forces and bases on their territory. For example, I would understand a British policy of excluding Americans from the British Isles in the event of an emergency. At present American bases located there may not precipitate a war and they may even serve as a so-called deterrent. In other words, the Soviet Union probably will not start military attacks until they have absolute assurance that they have supremacy, including the power to neutralize military installations in the British Isles. But I would like to remind you about an earlier statement I made this morning to the effect that in my judgment the Soviet leaders will not precipitate an all-out war.

Mr. ARENS. You mean a shooting war?

General WEDEMEYER. Yes, I do. It is my conviction that the Soviet Union will continue to intensify its efforts in the economic psychological, and political fields. Unless and until they are confronted with intelligent, coordinated action on our part in those same fields the Soviet Union will continue to enjoy success everywhere. They have the initiative now in all fields of strategy. I feel certain that they will not resort to the use of military force unless compelled to do so. Of course, gentlemen, no one can predict what might happen in a state with a chief executive like Khrushchev who I understand gets very drunk on occasion. If these reports be true, he could understandably be impulsive, arrogant, and at time irresponsible. In such a mood he might take precipitous action which would touch off a global war. However, under normal conditions in my judgment there will not be a shooting war for some time to come.

Mr. ARENS. How late is it on the Soviet timetable for world domination?

General WEDEMEYER. From our viewpoint?

Mr. ARENS. Yes, sir.

General WEDEMEYER. Several years ago when I was still in the military service I testified before a congressional committee to the effect that I thought it was then too late.

Mr. ARENS. Do you think it is too late now?

General WEDEMEYER. Yes, sir.

Mr. ARENS. That is your honest judgment, General, as a military man who has served his nation in the very top echelon of global planning?

General WEDEMEYER. Yes sir. That was my viewpoint several years ago when I testified before congressional committees to that effect. It is still my viewpoint. However, I am not completely pessimistic about our chances to recover a sufficiently strong strategic posture vis-à-vis the Soviet. If we make a careful analysis of all of the countries which endanger our position, evaluate their capabilities and their limitations, and then determine how much assistance, realistic or passive, that we might expect from allies, and finally consider our own potential strength, I think that we would find our position in the world is not without' hope, in fact we would be most optimistic if we could foresee the coordinated employment of all the positive forces that we have on our side to counter our potential enemies and to overcome obstacles offered by them to the attainment of our objectives. I have confidence in American ingenuity, in our courage, and in our capacity to plan intelligently if we are only provided the direction from responsible leaders. But we must bring about concerted action to attain our goals and stop the indiscriminate and uncoordinated use of our political, economic, psychological, and military forces.

Mr. ARENS. General, may I now invite your attention to each of the several principal areas of the world for your appraisal of the designs and objectives that the Soviets have in each of them. First of all, I invite your attention to the Middle East. What are the designs, objectives, techniques, and strategy of the international Communist operation there?

General WEDEMEYER. I have mentioned earlier, in fact repeatedly this morning, that every nation has four instruments of national policy available to use in connection with the attainment of its national objectives. I have also stated that the Soviet Union has used these instruments intelligently, and no doubt in consonance with an overall plan. As Congressman Kearney earlier pointed out in one of his questions, the Soviet Union has an objective. Furthermore, may I state that all of the subordinates in the Soviet Union are knowledgeable about and are working continuously, resort to any means, to attain those objectives. Now in applying these ideas to the Middle East in answer to Mr. Arens' pointed question, I think that the Soviet Union is determined to alienate Arab friendship for the western peoples. Militarily the Arab countries are not very important. Economically the Middle East is of great importance, particularly to the industries of Western Europe, for there exists in the Middle East the great reserve of black gold-oil. To deny oil to the western European countries of course would be a tremendous victory for Soviet objective of weakening the military and economic strength of the West. So the Soviet effort in the economic field will be marked by loans to Middle East nations, by making available sorely needed products, foodstuffs, machinery, and by negotiating favorable exchanges in order to alienate the trade of western countries and to win particularly the loyalty or at least the dependence or gratitude of the recipient or beneficiary nations and peoples throughout the Middle East. This emphasizes my contention that the Soviet will continue the present policy of avoiding an all-out war while employing to the utmost the economic weapons available to them. In the Middle East the Soviet could easily infiltrate the oil industries: and even the governments in Saudi Arabia, Iran, and Iraq, with a view to sabotaging the economic interests of western European countries. Favorable economic relations lead to advantages in the psychological field. As already mentioned, many people of the world feel grateful to the Soviet Union because they have been given foodstuffs, military arms, and other products, whereas they may have been refused this same economic or military aid by the United States. Egypt is a good example, having first applied to the United States for wheat which they wanted to buy and pay for from their own dollar account. I mentioned this case earlier today. The Soviet agents are clever in exploiting economic aid so that they derive the full psychological advantage.

Mr. ARENS. How about Africa?

General WEDEMEYER. In Africa we find undeveloped resources that are also important. As a matter of fact, only recently in the Sahara Desert oil has been discovered. It is this important commodity that is so strongly influencing the adamant attitude of the French with regard to giving complete autonomy to Algeria. In Africa also we find a strong wave of nationalism which renders the timeworn policy of colonialism obsolete or dangerous to pursue. It is in our self-interest to build up stable and friendly relations with the people of all races in Africa. Also we should be sympathetic to their desires for self-government. Militarily Africa affords many important air and naval bases favorably situated in the event of military action against the Soviet Union. Economically there are many products which are valuable to our own highly integrated industry including rubber, bauxite, magnesium, diamonds, ivory, cotton, and uranium. Incidentally, gentlemen, there is an excellent book entitled "Somewhere South of Suez" by Douglas Reed which describes the developments in Africa objectively and comprehensively.

Mr. ARENS. Do you believe that the Soviet Union in this drive for world domination is bypassing Western Europe and concentrating on the Middle East or Far East, or do you think that Western Europe plays a more important role in the Communist designs for world domination?

General WEDEMEYER. When a commander is planning his scheme of maneuver in combat, he tries to avoid strength and attack weakness. He conducts probing operations in order to discover weak areas and then maneuvers his forces in order to penetrate such areas. This provides the greatest chance of success and also will minimize losses. These tactics have been employed since time immemorial by all military commanders. The Soviet Union employs the same tactics in the use of economic, psychological, and political weapons as well as military. During World War II we all were aware of the fact that vacua would be created in the course of military operations. The wholesale killing, destruction, dislocations, and disruptions would naturally create these vacua and as soon as hostilities ended, some force would be drawn inevitably to fill them. Because we were naive or did not realize the true objectives of the Soviet Union we made no attempt to fill the vacua with our own forces. The communists poured in agents, provocateurs, saboteurs, and propagandists in order to exert the dominating influence in these war-torn areas. It was the American planners' hope in the early days of World War II, as I indicated earlier, that Anglo-American forces would be in a favorable position at war's end to fill those vacua and thus deny them to the Communists. It was the contention of the American planners that Anglo-American forces should go across the British Channel in 1943 and drive eastward as rapidly and as far as possible. It was felt that such a maneuver would be highly successful because the bulk of the German forces at that time (early 1943) were deeply and irretrievably committed far to the east in the vast expanse of Russia. But the persuasive and articulate British leader, Winston Churchill, successfully compelled the Allies to accept his strategy of scatterization or periphery pecking. Anglo-American forces executed time and force consuming and indecisive maneuvers in the Mediterranean. In the planning phase the Americans opposed such operations and in fact stated that even if Rommel could run rampant along the African coast it would not decisively affect the ultimate victory, provided the Allied effort concentrated on a drive toward the heartland of Germany. It was felt by the American planners that a concentration and employment of force for that purpose would have resulted in Anglo-American forces advancing eastward into the Balkans and at least halfway across Poland by war's end. Obviously if this had occurred, the Communists would not have been in a position to exercise their domination over eastern Germany, Poland, Czechoslovakia, and the Balkans in general. The whole map of Europe would be radically different today.

Mr. ARENS. What do you believe the strategy of the Soviet Union or Red bloc is in Germany today, General?

General WEDEXEYER. I am sorry, Mr. Arens, you asked that question, although phrased differently, just a few minutes ago and yet I have not answered it completely.

Mr. ARENS. The essence of my question was "Are the Soviet plans bypassing Europe?"

General WEDEMEYER. I believe that they would bypass Europe if by going elsewhere advantages would accrue to their world communization objective. For example, if they find weaknesses or soft spots in Southeast Asia, specifically in Indonesia, they would intensify their efforts in that area. If it develops that labor unrest occurs on a large scale in the South American countries, the Soviet would take advantage of such weaknesses there and would give impetus to the unrest in divers and insidious ways. As I stated previously, any strategic plan should be flexible so that the weaknesses of an opponent can be exploited. Whenever an opportunity is presented to use aggressively any or all of the four instruments of national policy, this should be done. I think the Soviet Union has followed such stratagem very effectively the past 10 years.

Mr. KEARNEY. Pardon me, General, but as you mentioned a minute ago in drawing up plans for an attack, the Soviet is continuously probing here and there to discover weaknesses, whether they be in the Middle East, Africa, or Europe?

General WEDEMEYER. That is correct, sir.

Mr. KEARNEY. They continually probe and then promptly exploit the weaknesses that they discover?

General WEDEMEYER. Yes, sir.

Mr. ARENS. General, may I direct your attention to the Far East in which we all know you served with great distinction for some considerable period of time.

Would you kindly give your appraisal of the designs of the Red leaders there. What can be expected from the standpoint of their strategy or tactics? Please give us any other observations that you think would be helpful in this connection to the committee and via this committee, to the American people.

General WEDEMEYER. I do not believe that the majority of the Chinese understood the full and sinister implications of communism when World War II came to an end. With equal conviction, I am sure that they did not understand the meaning of democracy. One must not forget that the bulk of the Chinese people are illiterate. The cultured Chinese with whom we come in contact are a very thin minority, perhaps a few million in a population exceeding 450 million. The Chinese people, that is the masses who are preponderantly peasants, are lovable, honest, energetic, and extremely loyal, particularly to their families. They respect authority and are warmly hospitable. The family unit is nurtured and older people are highly respected; also constituted authority is deferred to or obeyed. In other words, China is a country of peaceful, friendly, cooperative people. The Communist propaganda that was so successfully employed in that vast area became extremely vitriolic in the latter days of the war. Every morning on my desk I would find reports of monitored radio broadcasts emanating from Vladivostok, Moscow, and Yenan. The major theme of these broadcasts was arousing the suspicions and fanning hatreds of the Chinese against Americans. It was done very cleverly, emphasizing particularly that we Americans were in the area, remaining in order to exploit the poor people of China and that we had every intention of subjugating them in our own selfish interests. I reported these facts concerning Soviet propaganda in the China area to the Joint Chiefs of Staff who were my bosses back in the States. I was informed that such information was forwarded to the State Department. I also contacted the Soviet Ambassador in Chungking and remonstrated strongly and tactfully. The Ambassador' disclaimed any knowledge of the venomous propaganda to which I referred. He was very polite and firm in his denunciation of such methods, assuring me that the Soviet Union respected the United States and was a very loyal ally. Oddly enough, the denunciatory broadcasts discontinued for a while but resumed with even greater intensity and violence when the Japanese surrendered. My headquarters were located in Shanghai after the Jas surrendered. I again visited the senior Soviet official and provided him with a certified copy of the broadcasts. He too was most apologetic about the whole matter and assured me that the broadcasts must have their genesis in Yenan and stated categorically that the Soviet Government had no official connection with them. The Chinese people heard daily, in fact hourly, these radio broadcasts which were widespread and which urged the Chinese to compel the Yankees to get out of the Orient, in fact suggested that all white people be driven out of the Orient, repeating over and over again the theme "the Orient for Orientals." Many years before World War II the Soviet Union had established the Sun Yat-sen University in Moscow. This university was the training -around for the Chinese Communist leaders who are now so effective in organizing the people and inflaming them against the Nationalist Government as well as against Americans. These Chinese Communist leaders, including Chou En-lai, Mao Tse-tung, Chu Teh, and other prominent members of the Red party in China, received their basic training in socialism, subversion, propaganda, organization, and distortions of the truth under the tutelage of the Russian Communists. Actually, in 1945 at war's end, the Chinese Communists had very little power and were numerically insignificant. However, their propaganda was increasingly effective and was not only inspired but was actually supported and supplemented by the Soviet Communists. On our side, that is, the American cause or the Nationalist Chinese Government cause was not presented. Yet there was every opportunity to refute the Communist lies and to put the record straight, particularly with the masses of Chinese people. I tried to enlist the support of American diplomatic officials in China and also submitted reports to responsible officials back in Washington. The war was over and the people were celebrating victory. There was little or no interest or sympathetic understanding of the situation in China. There was strong pressure on all theater commanders to return the soldiers back to the homeland. No one seemed to be thinking in terms of protecting our hard-earned victory. You gentlemen on this congressional committee would be astounded if you could read the letters that I received when serving as theater commander in China, particularly at the end of the war. Many of them were disrespectful, derisive, and critical. Most of them conveyed the idea that I wanted to maintain a wartime rank and therefore would not permit the demobilization of my American forces in China. Just as rapidly as men acquired the number of points decided upon by higher authority to justify their evacuation to the homeland, I insisted that they be put on ships and sent to the United States. In doing this, often the organizational integrity and of course the overall efficiency of my command was greatly weakened. I read reports about rioting in some of the theaters because the GI's were becoming restive in waiting for the accumulation of the number of points that would entitle them to be sent to their homes. I believe there was some rioting in Manila and also in Frankfurt, Germany, but fortunately we did not have such a situation in China.

(At this point, Representative Walter entered the room.)

Mr. KEARNEY. There was some rioting in Hawaii too; was there not, General?

General WEDEMEYER. I believe so, sir.

Mr. KEARNEY. I recall the situation in Guam where, although we did not have any riots on the part of the GI's there, I received hundreds of letters from members of the Armed Forces located on that island and the gist of their message was "No boats, no votes."

General WEDEXEYER. Returning to the situation prevailing in China immediately after the war (1945), I noted a buildup of opposition against Chiang Kai-shek, the leader of the Nationalist Government. Criticism of the Generalissimo and his government frequently appeared in the press and was heard on the radio. Obviously if the Generalissimo had been the tyrant that the Communists, both in our country and in other areas, claimed he was, the press and radio would have been controlled. Certainly the Generalissimo could have done this just as easily as it is done in the Soviet Union and in other Communist dominated states. He chose to permit the people to express themselves freely. He was making an earnest effort to be a truly democratic leader. Some of the intellectual Chinese had affiliated themselves with communism and gradually others who were worried about their selfish interests decided to go over with the Communists because they felt that the Nationalist Government would be overthrown and they wanted to be on the winning side. General Marshall arrived as the special envoy of the President in December of 1945. It seems that Chiang Kai-shek had had only one prior contact with the former Chief of Staff and that was at the Cairo Conference. The Generalissimo seemed quite concerned about Marshall's arrival and queried me several times with reference to what Marshall would want to know and see, and what the real purpose of his visit might be. I was laudatory in my remarks concerning Marshall's capabilities, integrity, and earnest desire to help the Nationalist Government. After Marshall arrived he showed me his directive, which required him to amalgamate all of the various political fragments or parties in China. Perhaps I should indicate that in my several years of contact with General Marshall prior to service in China I had formed the highest regard for him and felt that I could at all times frankly disagree with his views and that my own approach to a problem would be considered in good faith by him. Of course I was respectful but not subservient and he encouraged such attitude. Therefore, when I read his directive from the State Department requiring him to bring together the conflicting parties, I told him frankly that he could not accomplish this. I explained that the Communists had very little power at that time (December 1945) but they were determined to get all of it. On the other hand the Nationalist Government had most of the power and they were equally determined not to

41

relinquish one iota of it. Numerically the Communists were greatly inferior. It is difficult to estimate exactly how many Chinese had affiliated themselves with the Communist movement. There were extravagant claims of course by the leaders, and some of our own Americans who were sympathetic to the Communists made rather stupidly high estimates. I think at the most a few million out of the total of more than 450 million people had varying degrees of loyalty to the Communist cause. Most of the hard core of the Chinese Communist movement was located in the province of Yenan. Regardless of what you gentlemen may have read or heard, I believe that I was in a position to state factually that the Communist troops did not contribute realistically or appreciably to the war effort against the Japanese. I was on the ground and certainly would have known if their claims that they were the real fighters against the Japs had been correct. As a matter of fact, I tried to bring about coordination of effort between the Nationalist and Communist forces but it was perfectly obvious that the Communist leaders were biding their time. I am equally sure that they had promises of support from the Soviet Communists when the propitious time arrived for them to begin their attacks against the Nationalist Government. The Chinese Communists were constantly requesting arms and equipment. My directive required me to support the Nationalist Government of China. Some of my political advisers did point out that these men were Chinese and that they were fighting effectively against the Japanese. I stated earlier that my efforts to -bring about a modicum of military assistance from the Communist forces were unsuccessful. They had some arms and equipment and all that I asked them to do was to exert pressure against the Japanese forces who were operating in the vicinity of Yenan. They refused to do this but would occasionally make sorties against a Japanese blockhouse or outpost, seizing a few prisoners, arms, and equipment but not making a real contribution to the overall war effort of the China theater. Chou En-lai reported to me that there was an epidemic in Yenan and requested medical supplies. Although I had repeatedly refused to send military equipment to them, I did send 11 tons of medical supplies into the Communist area. This was done with the cognizance and approval of Generalissimo Chiang Kai-shek and was recognized as a humanitarian step. When General Marshall arrived in China on his special mission for the President (1945), of course the war was over and the repatriation of millions of people who had moved into the hinterland during the Japanese occupation and the rehabilitation of war-stricken areas presented serious problems for the Generalissimo and his Government. The Chinese Communists supported by the Soviet Union spread their propaganda and intensified their activities to subvert the Nationalist military forces. The people, war-weary and confused, were taken in by the promises of the Communists for better opportunities, for food and land, all of which the Soviet propaganda emphasized. It never occurred to these simple, gullible people that the Chinese Communists neither had the capability nor the intention of fulfilling their promises. Also, the Chinese Communist propaganda distorted the situation so much that the people in the United States interpreted the conditions in China incorrectly. Chiang Kai-shek was depicted as an unscrupulous dictator whereas actually the man was trying to bring order out of chaos and still follow democratic procedures. There was much wrong in the government and there were dishonest and incompetent men m key positions. We here in America sometimes experience these same conditions in our own official ranks.

Mr. ARENS. What is your present appraisal of the posture of international communism in the Far East?

General WEDEMEYER. The Communists have the initiative throughout the Far East. The degree will vary, of course, in different areas but on the mainland of China they definitely have the upper hand. Economics will be an important factor in the outcome of the struggle in that area between the forces of freedom and those of enslavement. Traditionally the Japanese have carried on heavy trade with mainland China. They would obtain their raw materials from that area, ship them back to Japan which was highly industrialized, process these raw materials, and then send them back as finished products to markets throughout the Far East, again principally in China. Japanese processed goods are shipped to other markets but they experience difficulties because their products are so low-priced and inject a competition difficulty in countries where labor costs are higher, for example in the United States. But the overall picture of the Communists in the Far East is in my judgment favorable for continued Communist expansion and retention of the initiative unless and until confronted by a strong, realistic concerted effort in the political, economic, and psychological field by the so-called free nations of the world, principally the United States, Great Britain, and Japan.

Mr. ARENS. General, you have expressed yourself in an appraisal of the military, economic, psychological, and political superiority of the Red bloc in the world today.

How does this capability or superiority affect the relationship or posture of the United States with its allies and neutrals?

General WEDEMEYER. I mentioned a little earlier during the course of this hearing that in my judgment our allies will make realistic appraisals of the United States strength in all fields of strategy, and likewise of the Soviet Union. If an emergency occurs, I believe that our allies will estimate the situation and will take such steps or adopt such measures as will be in their own self-interest. Today they are accepting United States military and economic aid because it is in their self-interest. From a short-range viewpoint this would appear to be right. So far the Soviet Union has not reacted too strongly but some of these so-called allies are already making careful reappraisals and have agreed to carry on trade with Communist nations.

For example, some of our friends who strongly proclaim that they are opposed to communism and have even pledged support to us in the event of an emergency against Communist aggression are actively engaged in trade with Red countries. The British, for example, are trading with Red China. As far as I know, they gave diplomatic recognition to the Communist regime in China without consulting the United States. British trade has traditionally strongly influenced British policy in the field of diplomacy. If a wartime emergency should develop, I believe that the British would carefully analyze the implications of cooperating with us. They might decide to remain strictly neutral and thus deny us access to the military bases which we are now maintaining in the British Isles.

Mr. SCHERER. Deny us use of those bases?

General WEDEMEYER. Yes, sir. If I were a Frenchman, Britisher, or Spaniard and felt that it would be more advantageous to my country, I certainly would deny the use of the bases to the Americans. Of course, if the Americans had the upper hand or sufficient strength to assure me that they could defend my country against the Communist juggernaut, the Communist air armada, and a possible stream of destructive missiles, then probably I would consent to the use of the bases by the Americans. This is realism. All of the people in Europe want to be on the winning side in the next war. There is less desire to take calculated risks, partially due to the terrifying effect that the introduction of thermonuclear bombs and missiles has had on the people. Fortunately the Soviet leaders realize too that there will be no winning side in a nuclear war.

Mr. ARENS. Suppose Russia issued an ultimatum to the effect that if these countries allowed the Americans to use bases they would use nuclear intercontinental ballistic missiles on cities in England, Germany, France, and Spain?

General WEDEMEYER. The Soviets have already issued veiled ultimatums. The countries you mentioned are accepting calculated risks now. They feel that they can afford to do this because they still feel that the United States retaliatory powers would afford them protection. Also most of the people in Western Europe are quite certain that there will not be a war in the near future. The very destructive power inherent in new weapons may render their use unthinkable even to dictators. For these reasons the people of France, Spain, Germany, and England continue their collaboration with the United States. Also they are conscious of the fact that considerable economic and psychological advantage accrues by the presence of American bases in their countries. Our soldiers are spending millions of dollars in those countries. Furthermore, our Government spends considerable sums of money on the construction and maintenance of airdromes and the lines of communication, all of which will be valuable commercially to the countries concerned.

Mr. SCHERER. You refer, General, to the economic advantage such as the money we are spending in Asia?

General WEDEMEYER. Yes, Sir. I think all of the countries receiving aid from us are watching developments very carefully and weighing the implications of so doing. However, when the chips are down, I hope I am wrong, I think that these countries would be very reluctant allies and might consider seriously denying us the use of the bases which we are maintaining today. **I shall never forget the attitude of so-called allies and of the United Nations Organization when we, the United States, made an all-out effort in South Korea to stop the advance of the Red hordes from North Korea.** Everyone knows today that only two countries, South Korea and the United States, made a realistic contribution in that effort to stop the spread of communism.

Mr. KEARNEY. General, would I be wrong in supplementing Congressman Scherer's remarks by including every allied country in the Western World, not only the countries Congressman Scherer mentioned? I am trying to be realistic along with you and therefore have reference to every one of the countries when I ask you if they would stand by us in the event of trouble or in case war did break out. Don't you think that we would be left holding the bag, so to speak?

General WEDEMEYER. I believe that we would be left holding the bag, General Kearney, but again, I hope that I am wrong. However I have given this matter considerable thought over the years and have expressed to this committee my considered opinions.

Mr. SCHERER. I am a Member of Congress and have to vote on the expenditure of funds for more airfields and the maintenance of those airfields in England, Germany, France, and Spain that we already have. If what you say is true and I had come to the same conclusion before your testimony, General-how should I vote? Would it not be better to spend that money presently used on bases in other countries for submarines and long-range missiles that do not depend upon bases?

General WEDEMEYER. I would not vote one penny to any country unless I had evidence of their good faith and of their unswerving loyalty in the cooperative effort with us toward the attainment of common objectives; one important one, of course, is protecting the Free World against the scourge of communism. I am not suggesting that each one of these countries to whom we give military and economic aid should have exactly the same objectives in the international field, but I would insist that their objectives must be compatible with our own. In other words, if the British insist on trading with Red China and thus strengthening the Communists who present a grave danger to United States interests, then I would discontinue military or economic aid to the British. When I make a statement like that, Britishers and American "one-worlders" will say that they are not trading in strategic items. When they use the term "strategic items," they mean, of course, airplanes, tanks, ammunition, I presume. But I insist that any item of trade - a spool of thread, wheat, automobiles, or coffee - assists the economy of Red China. I believe in denying those areas under Communist rule any economic or military assistance. Furthermore I would break off diplomatic relations with them. In suggesting these ideas to the committee, I wish to emphasize that I am not an isolationist. No country can isolate itself from the world today. If this be a fact, the United States should participate in international developments and relations with intelligence, always mindful of the fact that we must be actuated by self-respect. In other words, every step that we take should protect our security and our economy. Let us be realistic and understand that all other countries conduct their foreign policies in that manner.

Mr. SCHERER. I understood that at the beginning of your testimony, General, you estimated the total firepower of the East and West to be about equally balanced, with possibly the East having a little edge at this time?

General WEDEMEYER. When you refer to firepower, I presume you mean military potential or military posture?

Mr. SCHERER. That is what I mean.

General WEDEMEYER. In my judgment the military strength or posture of the Soviet Union and satellites is stronger than that of the western countries or Free World.

Mr. SCHERER. Then if this is a fact and Russia says, as she has hinted to England and France, "The Americans must not use bases on your soil, and if you do permit them to do so, there will be a nuclear war waged against your cities," do you think for a minute that England and France would permit us to use these bases?

General WEDEMEYER. I doubt it very much. As you have suggested, the Soviet Communists have hinted that to several countries. I am sure the British are definitely worried about it. But again, trade is an important factor in the British philosophy. They probably are weighing all of the implications and, as we all know today, they are willing to accept the calculated risks involved. They must be evaluating all of the factors, principally that the Russians in all probability will not precipitate a war while they are enjoying such outstanding success in the use of economic and psychological weapons. The British are conscious of the fact that we Americans are spending a lot of money in their country and the door to our Treasury has long been ajar.

Mr. SCHERER. Then we might as well keep the money coming.

General WEDEMEYER. Yes, sir. Macmillan's government is accepting a calculated risk and I think will continue to do so. I believe a Labor government would discontinue the use of bases by Americans. But again, I emphasize that if the chips were down and Macmillan did not feel that we Americans could prevent the Soviet from pouring missiles into his industrial and populated areas, he might declare a neutral position and in the process, of course, deny us the use of bases in the British Isles. Perhaps Macmillan feels that there will be no war-particularly no thermonuclear bombs and missiles.

Mr. SCHERER. You take almost the same point of view as Gen. Bonner Fellers.

General WEDEMEYER. I did not know that Gen. Bonner Fellers had expressed similar views but I am not surprised. Many other generals and admirals and many private citizens would express similar views I am sure. I have high regard for General Fellers' judgment in the field of strategy.

Mr. KEARNEY. Following Congressman Scherer's line, General, what I cannot get through my head is this: Assuming that England and the rest of the allies are wavering between the calculated risk you mentioned and the moneys we are pouring in there, and knowing Russia as they do-that they can't trust them or trust their word-where do we come back to then?

General WEDEMEYER. I can't answer that question, General Kearney. One of the hopes for mankind, I think, was expressed by Congressman Scherer a little earlier. Within the satellite countries of Russia and throughout the Soviet Union there are ferments and defections building up. Human beings will not endure subordination to the iron heel of tyranny for an indefinite time. The answer to our present dilemma may be essentially provided by uprisings and finally the overthrow of the tyrants behind the Iron Curtain.

Mr. KEARNEY. I think as far as that statement is concerned that we Americans are just going along with wishful thinking. We have been hoping that there would be a revolution in the satellite countries for many years. The nearest that it has come was in Hungary.

General WEDEMEYER. That is right. The Hungarians were truly fighting for freedom. It is interesting to note that the front fighters in their effort to overthrow their oppressors in Hungary were not older people who had enjoyed freedom many years ago but it was the young men and women who had been exposed to Communist propaganda and false promises since World War II who led the revolt. And as this revolutionary movement in Hungary progressed, I asked myself, where are the Kosciuskos, the Pulaskis, and the Lafayettes of this or of any other free country? When we were fighting for our freedom here in America, those patriots came to our shores, endured hardships, and experienced dangers to help us attain our liberty. Why didn't some American general, or a military leader from England or France, go to the Hungarians and offer his services? There was not one professional military man like myself who made himself available. Why am I not willing to take risks and to experience hardships as did the men who fought so gallantly and selflessly shoulder to shoulder with our forefathers in this country? I am serious. I have given considerable thought to this situation. Are we real patriots? Are we dedicated to liberty? Are we getting soft?

Mr. SCHERER. Perhaps you would not have been permitted to do so.

General WEDEMEYER. If I were determined, I certainly could have reached Hungary and offered my assistance to those fighters for freedom.

Mr. KEARNEY. There was a poll taken in every civilized country in the world as to whether or not that particular nation would assist any of the Soviet satellites that might defect or carry on a revolution. Every country voted overwhelmingly "No."

General WEDEMEYER. The frightening possibility of a nuclear war seems to hang like a pall over the world-paralyzing actions that might precipitate war. I think if a poll were taken in England today and if such poll were conducted without any duress, the British people would vote to move our bases out of their country.

The CHAIRMAN. Doesn't that all stem from the terrific nationalist feeling in each of the nations?

General WEDEMEYER. Yes, sir. I think the existence or development of nationalist feeling has a very strong influence in this connection. It is an interesting phenomenon-our policies at home seem to favor and support internationalism-while abroad we support nationalism, the principle of self-determination.

The CHAIRMAN. I was in Yugoslavia sometime ago in connection with the refugee problems and talked with officials of the Yugoslav Government. They hate the Russians in my judgment just as much as we do but they are realistic to the point that I am concerned lest what we do to aid Yugoslavia would sometime or other be used against us if it was expedient to do so.

General WEDEMEYER. Tito and his henchmen are avowed Communists opposed to everything we stand for. Why strengthen his position economically or militarily with American aid?

Mr. SCHERER. That is why I am afraid these airbases in some of our neutral and allied countries will be used against us.

General WEDEMEYER. Congressman Scherer, related to your concern in this matter, when you cast your vote for appropriations covering the installation and maintenance of bases, would it not be a good idea to bring out clearly the motives and actions of those allies who are not doing their proportionate share in the struggle against communism? Specifically, expose those nations in the North Atlantic Treaty Organization which are not providing their proportionate share of the military forces for the NATO defense. Everyone knows that certain countries in NATO agreed to provide a stipulated number of divisions and yet they are not fulfilling their commitment. They come asking us for help but they fail to keep faith with us in the firm agreements made ostensibly to stop aggressions by the Communists.

Mr. KEARNEY. The Korean war was an excellent example of this.

General WEDEMEYER. Yes, sir. I cannot understand why American leaders permit allies to ignore or abrogate commitments. I have lived abroad for approximately 20 years of my life. In my contacts with foreign peoples I found them to be kind and cooperative. But also, may I emphasize that they were always realistic. If they did something for me, they expected gratitude as well as something from me in return. I am convinced that if the British were in the position of giving aid to us, they would insure that we were cooperating to the fullest degree in the attainment of their objectives and in protecting their interests. Some people suggest that when we Americans give aid to a country that we should not attempt to interfere with that country's internal affairs. My approach would be entirely different. In the first place I would not give aid, military or economic, to any country that opposed America's aims in the international field. Also, I would expect the recipient countries to indicate what they were going to do with our aid and when. Furthermore I would require those countries to give evidence at least of supporting objectives compatible with our own. In general those are the tests that I would make in each instance before I would approve of economic or military aid for any nation.

Mr. SCHERER. We just have so much money to spend and if we don't reach a conclusion as just stated by you, General, we will ruin our economy.

General WEDEMEYER. That's exactly the way I feel about it. I think we should put our aid, military and economic, in those areas and those countries where it will do the most to provide military security and economic stability for America as well as for the recipient nation. The present administration is asking now for permission to increase the debt limit. If I were a Congressman, I would oppose such increase and would cut down on expenditures both at home and abroad-particularly abroad.

Mr. SCHERER. I repeat, we have just so much money to spend and if we don't come to the conclusion that there is a limit at some place to these enormous expenditures, we are going to ruin our own economy. If our situation is as precarious as you suggest concerning our overseas bases, then isn't Admiral Rickover right that we should take the money we do have available and concentrate it on the construction of submarines which are capable of launching nuclear weapons?

General WEDEMEYER. I am glad that you asked that question, Congressman Scherer. I agree that we should carefully evaluate the expenditure of our money in connection with military security. We should concentrate our effort on those weapons which will provide a full dollar's return in security for our country. In my judgment the atomic submarine with missile platform would be an important addition and would render us less dependent on precarious bases located in the territories of reluctant allies.

Mr. SCHERER. This would be much cheaper than foreign bases.

General WEDEMEYER. Yes, sir. Our forces could rendezvous at any designated place, discharge their missiles against hostile targets, and submerge, then reappear at another predetermined rendezvous for another attack.

Mr. SCHERER. One would not have to have permission to establish bases on foreign soil if we operated in that manner.

General WEDEMEYER. That is correct. Furthermore, there would be no bases to destroy when the enemy attempted to retaliate, and greater flexibility in the employment of our missiles would be provided.

Mr. SCHERER. Yes; the submarines as platforms for missiles would be moving and thus would not present a good target for the enemy.

General WEDEMEYER. Yes; that is very important. I believe that Congress should carefully consider the research and development programs which provide for atomic and thermonuclear weapons for missiles and submarines. I do not agree with those who advocate large ground forces. Also, I believe we should remove all United States ground forces now located on foreign soil. The people indigenous to those countries do not like foreigners, particularly in military uniform, present in their communities. They have a nationalistic feeling which is understandable and resent the presence of armed men from other countries. Of course, the political leaders will not express such views, but I am sure a poll would reveal that the people themselves would be glad to have our troops removed. Most important let the people indigenous to the area provide the manpower for the defense of their country. I am sure this would be a more satisfactory arrangement, and I expect the people of those countries do not want our Armed Forces on their soil.

Mr. KEARNEY. Except in time of war.

General WEDEMEYER. Yes; then they are glad to have us. Even then there are inevitable frictions. Although we were fighting shoulder to shoulder with the Chinese during World War II, there were understandable incidents and frictions between my forces and the Chinese. In general, however, the Chinese were cooperative and hospitable. To return to the matter of appropriations, which Congressman Scherer mentioned earlier, I think it is very difficult for a Congressman or for any private citizen to know exactly how and when to approve of military and economic aid to other countries. The leaders in our Government - in fact, all officials occupying key positions in the executive and legislative branches of our Government - are so weighed down and harassed by daily administrative matters it is hardly possible for them to investigate, analyze, and reach sound judgments concerning the complex situations in various parts of the world. It seems tome that we need a group of disinterested men who are not harassed with day-by-day administrative responsibilities but who would spend their time studying and analyzing world developments in order to submit sound recommendations to Congress. I think that Congress should make the decisions concerning our various commitments in the international arena. It is the Congress that truly represents the grassroots-the people throughout our country. The President and his appointees in the State Department do not necessarily reflect the basic ideas of the American people. Policy-making should be in the hands of those who are responsive to the thinking and the will of the people. Today you gentlemen on this committee asked me, a layman, to make suggestions concerning appropriations. I really do not feel fully qualified to make comprehensive recommendations because I lack factual information. It seems to me there is need for a group of men who will continuously study the international

situation based on factual and complete information concerning developments in all parts of the world. Such a group would have the responsibility of evaluating developments and their implications upon our own security and economic stability. After their evaluations they should make appropriate recommendations to the Members of Congress, and thus facilitate sound legislative action which would then not only be based on the best intelligence available but would also be supported by expert evaluations and judgments.

The CHAIRMAN. I have been informed that when the Japanese surrendered in Java after World War II, unlike other surrenders, they were required to leave their arms. Do you know anything about that?

General WEDEMEYFR. Mr. Congressman, Java was not in my theater during World War II but was under the British at the time of the Japanese surrender. Actually Admiral Mountbatten, who commanded the southeast Asia area, was responsible for Java. I do not know what happened but the Japanese in all areas were required by the orders issued by supreme commander, Allied Powers, to turn their arms over to the Allied commander nearest to them. In this connection, I had some difficulty with the British concerning the surrender arrangements at Hong Kong. The instructions that the Generalissimo and Lord Louis Mountbatten received and also that I received from the supreme commander Allied Powers (General Mac-Arthur), stipulated clearly that the Chinese would receive all surrenders of Japanese in the China theater. Hong Kong was in the China theater, yet the British insisted that they would not permit the Chinese to receive the surrender in Hong Kong. The Generalissimo asked me as his chief of staff to go to Hong Kong and accept the surrender of the Japanese commander there. I refused but recommended to the Generalissimo that a Chinese general be sent to Hong Kong and to other key points throughout China for that purpose. My reason was that it would be better psychologically for the Chinese to receive the surrender of the Japs whom they had been fighting for 8 years. In Nanking, in Shanghai, and in fact throughout the China theater I arranged to have a Chinese commander present at the surrender of the Japanese. But the British protested violently and even sent messages to President Truman claiming that it was their right and responsibility to receive the surrender of the Japanese in Hong Kong. They were arrogant and disrespectful to the Generalissimo in handling this matter. I was surprised and disappointed that they should be so petty in this matter of protocol. After all, the Chinese had fought 8 years against the Japanese and had made great sacrifice in carrying on against the common enemy. The matter ended up with the British receiving the surrender. They rushed an admiral there for that purpose along with a few of their combat ships which had been operating in the Bay of Bengal during most of the war.

The CHAIRMAN. The thing that disturbs me as one of the most serious situations in the world today is that which is developing in Indonesia.

General WEDEMEYER. Yes

The CHAIRMAN. I can just imagine what would happen if a Communist state were to develop in Indonesia, situated there between the Philippines, Japan, and Australia.

General WEDEMEYER. Yes; that is quite true. Communism apparently is developing quite strongly in Malaya also.

The CHAIRMAN. Yes, and I do not think it was a mere accident that the surrender there in Malaya was different than anywhere else; in other words, the Japanese went away with their arms. In Indonesia, the Japanese turned over their arms to pro-Communists.

General WEDEMEYER. As another indication of Communist influence in those areas, it is reported that in Okinawa recently a mayor was elected with pro-Communist leanings.

Mr. ARENS. General, you have given us an appraisal of the rising strength of the Red bloc in the military, economic, psychological, and political fields as well as the threat which the Communist bloc poses to the Free World. Would you care to give your appraisal to this committee of any mistakes which have been made by the West and your suggestion as to a strategy or tactic of the West to counter the rising tide of the Red bloc?

General WEDEMEYER. Our failures were due to the fact that we did not recognize the true implications of international communism during and particularly subsequent to World War II. I think the fact that we were so trusting and naive after World War II concerning the sinister motives of the Communist leaders was the most serious blunder that western diplomats and western leaders made.

Mr. ARENS. How did that affect the situation?

General WEDEMEYER. Well, this enabled the Soviet to maintain the initiative in Europe as well as in the Far East. They had complete initiative in the political, economic, and psychological fields and thus extended their influence throughout those areas, drawing successfully into the poisonous orbit of communism countries and millions of people.

Mr. ARENS. What are the manifestations in your opinion of this failure to recognize the nature of international communism?

General WEDEMEYER. I might give a few examples Let us recall the situation that developed in Czechoslovakia where the Soviet moved in surreptitiously after the war. It was not a military operation. Communist agents obtained positions in the Government. They gradually took over the control of the Interior Department which was responsible for the internal security of the country. The secret police in Czechoslovakia operated within the Interior Department. When the Communists obtained control over that Department, obviously they could take over the entire Government. That was exactly what they did. The Communists have not employed their own troops that is, their army, navy, or air force, in any major military action since World War II but they have been very successful in implementing troops of satellites in gaining control of vast areas and many countries. For example, Red China, North Korea, Poland, Albania, Czechoslovakia, East Germany, Hungary, Bulgaria, Rumania. About half the population of the world, over a billion people, are now oriented toward the Kremlin, and this nonmilitary but effective method of taking over the control of countries was accomplished without effective opposition on our part or on the part of the U. N. The western countries ignored Communist aggressions while they concentrated on the rehabilitation of their own countries after the war. Furthermore the western countries have had continuous difficulty in adopting an honest, unified position vis-à-vis the Soviet Union. However, they were all doing their utmost to get as much as they could in the form of United States military and economic aid. The Communists brazenly violated their agreements made with the western countries and of course made a mockery of the humane and enlightened Charter of the United Nations.

Mr. ARENS. What suggestion do you make, General, for a strategy of the West to cope with this threat of international communism?

General WEDEMEYER. **I think the most important thing is education. All of our people and people of the world should be given factual information concerning communism. If the American people had been told the truth in an unemotional and objective manner about Marx, Stalin, Lenin, and other Communists, they would have compelled their own leaders to take appropriate action. When the American people know what is going on, they always have exercised good judgment, I think they would support programs of firm, realistic action against Communist aggressions and penetrations. As I travel around in our country and in other parts of the world, I still find a lack of understanding of the problems presented by international communism. Most people don't**

understand the problem in China or in Hungary. Many people are woefully ignorant about international affairs. This is sometimes due to their inability to obtain factual information. Often, too, it is due to apathy or indifference. I recently had some dental work done. The doctor was an excellent dentist and did a very fine job. He discussed headlines that he had read in the newspaper, which revealed startling ignorance concerning communism. He is not at all left wing or communistically inclined but he is definitely naive about the motives of Khrushchev and Bulganin. It seems to me education is of paramount importance. The American people must be given simple truths-for example, that communism is not a political philosophy-the Communist Party is not at all like our Republican or Democratic Party. **The Communist Party is determined to subjugate the world and will resort to murder, lies, slave camps, in fact any means will be employed to remove obstacles and opponents to their ruthless plans. Communism must be recognized as exactly what it is-an international conspiracy to destroy faith in God, faith in mankind, faith in our form of government. In other words, it is dedicated to the destruction of religious, political, social, and economic freedoms.** My dentist friend explained that he had little time to read but did refer to an article he had just read in a magazine. I recognized at once that this magazine has been far left of center.

The CHAIRMAN. You mean "liberal"?

General WEDEMEYER. Well, in a sense I do, Mr. Congressman. However, I think both you and I are true "liberals," and that word has been bandied about so much it is difficult to know exactly what is meant when one uses the term. Personally I am always interested in what motivates people who write such articles.

Mr. DOYLE. May I inquire of the general before the bell rings – did you state positively that the Soviets will communize the world, in your judgment?

General WEDEMEYER. No. I didn't state positively that the Soviets would communize the world and I'm sorry that I gave you that impression. I stated, sir, that at this time **they have the initiative in the political, economic, and psychological fields, and, of course, we all know that their objective is to communize the world.**

Mr. DOYLE. In all fields of strategy they have the initiative?

General WEDEMEYER. Yes, sir; they do. In my opinion **they are gradually gaining in the accomplishment of their objectives. In other words, they are gradually exercising greater influence in all countries of the world, including our own.**

Mr. DOYLE. They do not intend to precipitate a world war?

General WEDEMEYER. I repeat, Mr. Congressman, I do not think that they intend to use military force as an instrument of national policy at this time. Why should they when they are successful in using the other three important instruments of national policy; namely, political, economic, and psychological?

Mr. SCHERER. Do you think they will use military force in the immediate future?

General WEDEMEYER. No; I don't believe that they intend to use military force in the foreseeable future.

Mr. DOYLE. I didn't preface my question in a way to cross-examine you.

General WEDEMEYER. I understand, sir.

Mr. DOYLE. You have been conferring with Mr. Arens and our staff as consultant. In relating these experiences that you have had I note that they do not pertain to a specific political party. In other words, the failures to handle the problems created by communism do not seem to attach to a particular political party but you associate those events with the party that happened to be in the White House at the time. Is that correct?

General WEDEMEYER. Yes, sir. **I have not had any particular political party or any individual in mind as I answered questions this morning. I would say that both the Republicans and the Democrats are equally culpable**.

Mr. DOYLE. I would like now to come down to us here in Congress. This committee for instance and the Subversive Activities Control Board have certain responsibilities to Congress. What have you to recommend that we do immediately in our field of responsibility something that we can actually touch and reach?

General WEDEMEYER. Yes, sir, I believe I understand. I know there is an aversion to the creation of more committees and more special bureaus; but I think that the assignment and hoped-for results of the committee that I suggest would be of tremendous help to Congress, as well as to the Executive, in reaching sound solutions to the complex problems facing our Nation. Such a group would comprise economists, historians, political scientists, educators, industrialists, bankers, farmers-men who have had varied and broad experience in life. This group would continuously study international developments. This would require a thorough examination of Communist methods, Communist operations, and appropriate recommendations could be provided to the Congress and to responsible leaders of our Government.

Mr. DOYLE. You have heard, of course, about the Rockefeller committee which recently submitted a report.

General WEDEMEYER. Yes; I read about Mr. Rockefeller's group.

Mr. DOYLE. There are many dedicated citizens who have studied these problems, that is, individuals outside of Congress.

General WEDEMEYER. Yes, sir. However, they have no authority, no official status. They might make excellent recommendations but the are not heeded. If we had a group such as I described working under the aegis of Congress, I believe sound counsel and recommendations would emerge as the basis for appropriate legislation to cope realistically with communism, both at home and abroad.

Mr. DOYLE. But the President has such committees now and he has so announced.

General WEDEMEYER. I did not realize that the President had a committee specifically for such purpose.

Mr. DOYLE. Yes, he has named 2 or 3 advisory committees and also he has the National Security Council which should provide appropriate recommendations.

General WEDEMEYER. Does the Congress have access to the information provided the National Security Council I

Mr. DOYLE. No.

General WEDEMEYER. I think the Members of Congress should be given the pertinent information collected by our intelligence agencies - by the Central Intelligence

Agency and by the intelligence representatives of the three military services. How can one form intelligent judgments without timely and factual information? We need courage and honesty, as well as intelligence, in our ranks. The advice and recommendations given to our leaders and to Members of Congress must be based on real knowledge and/or personal experience. We should avoid the counsel of individuals who would be in any way influenced by political expediency, personal popularity, or selfish interests. Guts, courage, integrity, intelligence must characterize our defense of liberty or we'll lose it.

Mr. DOYLE. General, I didn't lay the foundation for the information that I was apparently seeking. In other words, I am primarily thinking of our Committee on Un-American Activities. The problem we have in our Nation of meeting **the Communist threat - the subversive threat.** Have you had time to form any recommendations on that?

General WEDEMEYER. Sir, I think you are now doing a very constructive job, namely, calling in so-called experts in various linesmen and women who had some experience with communism - to give you the benefit of their knowledge and experience. The information that you receive from the many witnesses who appear here should help you in formulating plans and in recommending appropriate legislation to cope with the Communists and related problems.

The CHAIRMAN. For the majority of the committee I will answer that in the affirmative. That is what we are trying to do.

General WEDEMEYER. I think you are doing a very fine job. I do read most of the material published by this committee.

Mr. DOYLE. So do I think we are doing a pretty good job? Don't misunderstand me. I am always on the search, however, for the considered opinion of men who are on the outside looking at us objectively and apparently making a nonofficial appraisal of our national problem resulting from Communist subversion. That is what I am after, In other words, I am in search for that particular thing because that is the area in which presently I am officially responsible as a member of this committee.

General WEDEMEYER. I have no additional recommendations to make. As I stated before, I am reading the material which is published by this committee. I am certain that the members are carefully evaluating the information that they receive and that they will initiate appropriate legislation at the propitious time. I think there has been a gradual improvement in the past 10 years in connection with alerting our fellow Americans to the dangers of communism. I still would like to see an even greater effort made. Mr. Doyle, were you in Congress approximately 10 years ago, that is, immediately after World War II?

Mr. Doyle. Yes; I have been here about 12 years.

General WEDEMEYER. Then you may recall the situation that existed in this country, in fact throughout the world immediately after World War II. We were very trusting here in America concerning the Kremlin and its policies and actions. Our approach was naive, and, as a matter of fact, in some quarters, we were very enthusiastic about the Soviet leaders and people. We had defeated the Germans and Italians in Europe and the Japanese in the Far East. We all wanted to celebrate the victory and to live in peace.   It would have been impossible, to convince most of our fellow Americans that there could be **another threat even greater than nazism, and that this very threat existed in the Soviet Union.**

The CHAIRMAN. That very thing was made capital of by the people who were and are our enemies. They took advantage of our friend attitude.

Mr. DOYLE. General I take it that in your opinion there is no question but that the Soviet Union intends economically, politically and psychologically, and if need be militarily to conquer the world.

General WEDEMEYER. That is correct, Mr. Congressman. There is no doubt in my mind that the Soviet Union, under present circumstances and leadership, is committed to those objectives. They are steeped in the principles of Marxism which have never changed, but the methods of applying have been changed and switched about in whatever manner would promise success. The people behind the Iron Curtain have had approximately two generations of the Big Lie-hate, propaganda, distortion of facts, slave camps, police state restrictions, and military oppression. When I lived in Germany during the years 1936-38, I observed the manner in which the young people were indoctrinated by the Nazis. The Communists use similar methods, even more effectively. Factual information is excluded from everyone. The children are gathered together at an early impressionable age and subjected to propaganda of hate and suspicion against other countries. Most of these young people become fanatic believers in communism - it is almost a religion with them. Imagine after several generations have passed with this type of indoctrination, excluding the truth, distorting history-the effect upon the masses of people behind the Iron Curtain.

Mr. DOYLE. That applies, you mean, to the younger generation in Russia too?

General WEDEMEYER. Exactly. Yes, sir.

Mr. DOYLE. I think that is right.

General WEDEMEYER. Yes, the Russian children are being indoctrinated to believe in the righteousness of their cause, that any means justifies the attainment of the Soviet objectives. Kill, lie, distort, torture - all are fully justified in the Soviet conscience because they are so dedicated to the attainment of Marxian, Leninist, or Stalinist objectives.

Mr. DOYLE. Thank you very much, General.

Mr. ARENS. Mr. Chairman, we have no further questions.

The CHAIRMAN. I have none.

General WEDEMEYER. I have never met Congressman Walter before but knew Senator McCarran quite well, and admired and respected him. I have read very carefully the Walter-McCarran Act pertaining to immigration. It is excellent legislation and should, in my considered opinion, be given a thorough and extended application before any modifications are accepted by the Congress. It may be that changing conditions later on would justify a few modifications, but I think in it would be a mistake to effect changes at the present time.

The CHAIRMAN. Of course we had in mind in drafting the act, and as you know it took us nearly 5 years to put together this measure, the best interests of the United States. We were subjected to pressures from all sides by all sorts of so-called minority groups. But, fortunately, we had two committees which withstood the pressures. General, on behalf of the committee-and I am sure of the entire Congress - I want to extend to you our thanks for this enlightening contribution. Too few people realize exactly the seriousness of this world situation. We in the United States are fortunate in having at our disposal, whether we use them properly or not, people who can supply the sort of information that will make it possible for this great Republic of ours to survive. I again extend to you our thanks.

General WEDEMEYER. Thank you, sir.

(Whereupon, at 11: 50 a. m., Tuesday, January 21, 1958, the committee was recessed, subject to call.)